T0196469

The Journey of a Believer

The *Journey* *of a* *Believer*

THE DESTINY OF A BELIEVER

James Ardis Burnell

WESTBOW
PRESS®
A DIVISION OF THOMAS NELSON
& ZONDERVAN

Copyright © 2017 James Ardis Burnell.

All rights reserved. No part of this book may be used or reproduced by any means, graphic, electronic, or mechanical, including photocopying, recording, taping or by any information storage retrieval system without the written permission of the author except in the case of brief quotations embodied in critical articles and reviews.

WestBow Press books may be ordered through booksellers or by contacting:

WestBow Press
A Division of Thomas Nelson & Zondervan
1663 Liberty Drive
Bloomington, IN 47403
www.westbowpress.com
1 (866) 928-1240

Because of the dynamic nature of the Internet, any web addresses or links contained in this book may have changed since publication and may no longer be valid. The views expressed in this work are solely those of the author and do not necessarily reflect the views of the publisher, and the publisher hereby disclaims any responsibility for them.

Any people depicted in stock imagery provided by Thinkstock are models, and such images are being used for illustrative purposes only.
Certain stock imagery © Thinkstock.

All scriptures are from the KING JAMES VERSION (KJV):
KING JAMES VERSION, public domain

ISBN: 978-1-5127-8470-1 (sc)
ISBN: 978-1-5127-8471-8 (e)

Library of Congress Control Number: 2017906142

Print information available on the last page.

WestBow Press rev. date: 4/18/2017

Preface

As an introduction to my upcoming new book about the saga of James A. Burnell, I thought I would whet your appetite about this very unassuming person called Pastor James A. Burnell. By the way, I did pastor for several years at the Center of Life and Truth in Los Angeles, California, at the corner of Forty-Sixth and Compton Avenue.

I copastored with my youngest sister, Pastor Wanda P. Scott, while under the great leadership of the late Bishop King Solomon Burke, who directed us, guided us, advised us, and counseled us in many spiritual things to enhance our personal leadership skills among the flock. It was a very dynamic period of my life, and I experienced personal growth and development as a minister of the gospel.

Under the leadership of Bishop King Solomon Burke, we did many things. For example, we regularly had a radio ministry and invited people for salvation and eventually water baptism. Many of my relatives were involved in our ministry at the Forty-Sixth and Compton location. Queen Mother Burnell was one of our missionaries, and she was always on fire for God!

Queen Mother Burnell was a seasoned church mother who had many years of experience and exposure to the spiritual world. As not only my biological mother but my spiritual mother, she was always very edifying, exalting, and encouraging of our programs at the church. We fed many, many people, and we encouraged many, many people to follow Jesus as their personal Lord and Savior.

What I liked about my personal relationship with the late Bishop King Solomon Burke was that he lived life very large. He was a rather large man. He was the godfather to my nieces and nephews. He loved people, especially children. King Bishop Solomon Burke had over twenty children of his own. We all loved him very much, hallelujah!

I do not know whether many people know that the late King Bishop Solomon Burke was a professional musician with a very melodious and velvet voice. He originated from Philadelphia, Pennsylvania, and in 2003, he was inducted into the Rock and Roll Hall of Fame. He is now walking the streets of glory and is in the Hall of Faith! Praise God.

*T*his memoir is *dedicated* to my late mother, Algerine Joe-Burnell, a wonderful missionary of the gospel for over fifty years. She was a marvelous soul winner for Jesus Christ!

She labored before the Lord for my personal salvation for fifteen years, or a decade and a half. I have since been a Christian for thirty years.

Introduction

My journey as a writer commenced one day in earnest. I was sitting in CCI, across the street from studio C, listening to Dr. Mark Chironna, who had flown in from Florida to do a taping. As he was recording and prophesying, he suddenly called me out of the audience and began to prophesy over me. It was back in June 2006, just over six years ago. It was quite an experience. It was supernatural and miraculous at the same time. Dr. Mark Chironna commenced to declare things over me that afternoon that virtually penetrated and overwhelmed me! First and foremost, he mentioned that I would eventually write a devotional book and generate quite a bit of finances in my own personal life! Let me digress from the subject matter and speak about how I came to be at CCI.

As an ABC prayer partner, I was supposed to be at studio C that day, but the bus broke down, and this prevented the audience from getting there. We all were rounded up and marched over to CCI, and we replaced them that marvelous and wonderful day! Many, many other TBN prayer partners heard Dr. Chironna prophesy these words and began to ask me when was I going to write this book!

Six years have passed, and I have yet to write my first sentence, let alone my first paragraph. During this time, I have done absolutely nothing—shame on me! In recent months, I have begun to talk with people who have taken the time and effort to put pen to paper to create a book. I decided, with the help of the Holy Spirit, to allow Him to get my creative juices flowing.

It is amazing what one can accomplish with pen and paper when God is at the epicenter of it all. Pen and paper are no stranger to me; as a matter of fact, we all get along very well. I have been writing speeches for over a third of a century as a Toastmaster. Since I began as a Toastmaster a third of a century ago, I wrote my first speech, all six minutes of it. It was an icebreaker: "My Journey West."

This is my first real attempt to write a book! It is not a devotional book as usual with the months, the days, and the hours, but perhaps my main focus will be a combination of my personal life, prayer partner life, and other experiences.

Anyway, getting back to my Toastmasters International experiences. Through this I have grown tremendously with my writing proclivity and communication ability. The name of the Toastmasters International Club was Century Club 100. It was chartered in September of 1938, fourteen years after Toastmasters had its inauguration. The club itself was eleven years and two months older than me! When I gave my first TI speech, there were about forty members present when I gave my icebreaker. What a joy; what an honor!

It was a morning club that represented various cultures, religions, races, etc. To my surprise, I did very well during my speech because, after all, it was about me—James Ardis Burnell. Little did I know that this would be my first speech of many, many more to follow. By the way, we also had many, many women members. After all, our club president was a woman named Marlene Board.

Larry Sternberg was one of our longest-standing members, since September of 1968. He was a Jewish man who was almost like a statesman, and he loved politics. He had a wife named Eleanor and two little poodles. He also had one son and one daughter, both married and parents themselves. I learned how to become a better Toastmaster because of Larry's example and conduct.

Chapter 1

The Inward Journey

I was very blessed, fortunate, and privileged to be born in a Christian family. In addition, I was very privileged and fortunate to be born in the United States in the middle of the twentieth century in the small town of Camden, Arkansas—not Camden, New Jersey. In other words, I was an Arkie or Razorback by birth. I spent my first seven years in the southwest of Arkansas.

These are what you call formative years: age zero to seven years old. During these critical and very vital years, I learned how to talk and walk. I must have learned to walk around nine to eighteen months. I happened to be child number eight—and boy number five. There were seven siblings above me and two beneath me. As you can see, there was long line of chain of command or pecking order! I was not aware of all of my siblings until much later. To me, I came from a three-core family. The first core was comprised of my older siblings Gene, Ruth, and Evelyn. The second core included Perry Jr., Beasley, and Charles, and the third core had Princess (Liz), James, John, and Wanda. This made a grand total of ten children: six boys and four girls. The first and second cores raised the third core; there was that much of an age gap between them. My older brother was at least sixteen years older than my baby sister and thirteen years older than my baby brother. So in essence, my older siblings were our surrogate parents since we were raised during the '40s and '50s. Obedience was no problem, in my opinion.

As a child, I could sense a spiritual presence within our family. It was especially obvious within our mother. She made it her responsibility and obligation to take all of her children to church with her. Every Sunday, we were in the church, sitting on the pews along with her. For some reason, children were seen and not heard back then.

I felt that this unseen Supreme Being had a divine and omnipotent hand on my tiny life. I felt that my mom must have dedicated me to the Lord at an early age before I reached accountability. I had this inner accountability to being obedient to both my mom and dad. I felt the inward working of God in my life at an early age.

Granted, we are spiritual beings living in physical bodies; therefore, our spirit resonates with the Supreme Being. I was not aware of my surroundings until I was at least five years old. For the first time, I realized that I lived on something called a farm-like environment or atmosphere. We had what we called a menagerie: chickens, dogs, cats, a horse, pigs, ducks, cows, etc. In essence, since I was born at home and delivered by a midwife, I felt that I was born in one era but lived in another: the biblical era. After all, my given name was James Ardis Burnell, and I had a younger brother named Johnnie Ray Burnell. What a revelation! There were only two years between my brother and me. We could have been called the sons of thunder because of our biblical names. Instead of the sons of Zeberdee, we could have been called the sons of Perry Sr.

John, my youngest brother, was a bit more adventuresome and eager to explore than me; he could be tempestuous or rambunctious because of his temperament! As we were growing up, we liked to horse around in a playful way. John just did not have a spiritual bent or proclivity. How did I know this? Simply because he never ever took to reading about spiritual things; they never were a part of his makeup. John was very intelligent about mechanical and physical things, but spiritual things he left alone.

After I spent my formative years in the south, our family decided to pull up stakes and move to the West Coast, where some of our other relatives lived. We came out west in stages. Since our dad already had a long-term job as a general helper at the paper mill, he elected to remain behind for nearly two years. He retired after two more years of service, which gave him twenty years.

My dad was not a believer. He never attended church with his family on Sunday until years later, when he truly became committed to Jesus Christ. Thank God for our godly mothers, who stayed the course over the years no matter how intense and powerful the spiritual warfare was. Romans 8:31 declares that if God is for you, who can be against you? When loved ones begin to act up and go astray, we don't know what to do to address the situation. That was hardly the case with missionary Algerine Joe Burnell, for she was a praying mother. There is no substitute for prayer. The old saying is no prayer, no power; little prayer, little power; much prayer, much power. Hallelujah!

My mother focused her prayers on me for the space of fifteen years so I would surrender my life to Christ. You didn't know missionary Burnell prays; no matter what it seemed like or looked like, she could lay down a barrage of prayer that would simply annihilate the enemy. If she wanted a specific child to come to the Lord, she got her desire met!

Anytime I found myself over at my parents' home, I would hear my mom praying for all of her children, especially me! She would intercede so loudly and deeply that it moved me to become very tearful and deeply convicted for fifteen years. My mother's prayers definitely impacted me for the kingdom of God. There is no other way to explain it.

When I was out into the world and doing worldly things, I felt those prayers of missionary Algerine Joe Burnell to such a degree that I seriously did not have a desire to become an alcoholic, drug addict, womanizer, etc. Occasionally, I would get caught up in various sins, such as fornication, drunkenness, and lying, from the time I officially left the Church of God in Christ (COGIC) and went into the world.

I was about eighteen years old when I stopped attending church in Santa Ana, California. At seventeen, I was baptized by the late Bishop Wilford Alexander of

COGIC. I felt that I was a genuine believer, but I had no one to disciple me. I learned the Twenty-Third Psalm and the Lord's Prayer (Matt. 6:9–13) and felt well fortified, but to my surprise, in 1968 I met some college students and started partying and drinking. There went my relationship with God.

In 1970, I was drafted by Uncle Sam into the US Army and eventually was sent not to Vietnam but to Europe. This is where I commenced to drink and party heavily. I loved to go out on the town. As an American GI, it got you a lot of attention. I went into a lot of places, such as bars, nightclubs, restaurants, and movies. Some of these places were off limits to American GIs, but we went anyway.

When I was stationed in Greece, I lived both on post and off post. I lived in downtown Kalameki, several miles outside of Athens. Most of the GIs were married or had live-in girlfriends. I chose not to have a live-in girlfriend but to date different women, and I had less trouble. I met a British girl named Gaynor. She was around twenty, and I was twenty-two. We went out and did a few things together at the beach, restaurants, and movies. Gaynor was about five feet seven and 135 pounds, with dark hair and hazel eyes. I did not know much about Gaynor. She liked to go to various Greek restaurants around Athens and Kalameki. I did not know her parents' names since she was from northern Europe but was now living in southern Europe as a tourist with a visa to stay in Greece, namely Athens.

Gaynor was a lot of fun to be around. I loved her British accent and her social personality. The British were very reserved people. By this, I mean they were not very emotional or demonstrative; they did not wear their emotions on their sleeves. The Greek women, however, were very demonstrative and emotional in their behavior, conduct, and attitude. But I found myself spending more time with Gaynor whenever I could. We would go to the beach sometimes. The Greek islands have some of the most beautiful beaches in the world. Gaynor was a very intelligent young lady!

Gaynor and her friend decided one summer to go from England to Greece by an Airbus 320, so they purchased a ticket and flew from England's Heathrow down to Athens. They spent the summer as tourists and sunbathing. I met Gaynor while visiting a friend off post. When we first met, we began to talk, and before we knew it, we started to do things together! There was a beach called Marathon Beach that was our favorite. We would go there and spend hours just walking around the beach. This, however, was a very wooded beach. It had many trees around it. I loved the secluded spots we went to. The water of the beach was crystal clear. People would come from all around the world, especially northern Europe, to visit Greece.

My only regret while in Greece was that I never visited the island of Rhodes. Although I have been to Greece twice, I never took the time to visit the Rhodes, so I cannot tell you much about that particular island. It was a tourist haven. I promise the next time I visit Greece, I will make certain that I visit the island of Rhodes.

I had visited a number of European countries, such as England. England, unlike Greece, was always overcast and dreary and very cold. The English were not the friendliest or most talkative. They pretty much stayed to themselves. They would call you "mate" sometimes as they reached out to you. England has a rich history; there were many old buildings, which were erected hundreds of years earlier. The English simply didn't believe in tearing things down as we Americans do! They simply built more! While in England, I visited Hyde Park, crossed the Thames River, walked past Buckingham Palace, and visited the British museum. To me, it was quite a sight to see. I never in all of my life thought of visiting England and all of its landscapes; what a joy, what an honor, what a privilege.

If you think the British or English were not too friendly, the French were very proud and arrogant people. If you don't know French, please do not go to France, especially Paris. Unless you have your own personal tour guide, it is going to be a long, long day. Make sure you purchase a little book on French so you can find your way around France. The only thing I liked about France was the countryside, not the people. They simply did not have time for you unless you spoke French fluently. Although I was not very well received by the French, I can say this: at least I have been there.

After visiting France, our next stop was Italy. What I liked about Italy was its ancient architecture and the design of the buildings. One warning: if you love photography and taking pictures, you had better keep your eyes on the camera or else it will disappear like magic: abracadabra! Other than that, I enjoyed eating pizza in Rome.

As a point of information, don't bring or carry a lot of suitcases or luggage with you as you travel around Europe. It will wear you down and keep you from enjoying your vacation. Travel light and smart. Take as little clothing with you as possible. There are laundromats in Europe where you can wash your clothes. Perhaps you can take a small suitcase and carry-on luggage. All you need to do is wash once in a while; you learn by experience. That is all there is to it.

I love to travel. I had no idea as a child that I would go to such countries as Germany, England, France, Italy, and Greece, let alone actually live in one. After taking stock of my personal life, I was convinced there is a God and I was personally accountable to him. I had no problem with the issue of sin being a major problem in my life, but I was yet unable to surrender to God. As a GI, I refused to attend church or read the Bible because I did not want to appear hypocritical or live a double life. As long as I was in the US Army, I did not attend church. I wanted to have fun. My attitude about fun was drinking and partying, and God was not a part of this scene. I could not serve mammon and God simultaneously (Matt. 6:24). It is amazing that our Lord is constantly convicting, not condemning, us of any of our sins.

All the while I was away from God, I knew it without a shadow of the doubt. It goes to show you that the prayers of the saints were steadily at work behind the scenes. That is why one must learn to take spiritual inventory of one's life if one is separated from God. I never had any problems believing whether there was a God. That part of my life was nonnegotiable because I just knew He existed. Without reading the Bible to confirm His existence, given the fact that I was born in a Christian home, this reinforced the existence of God. Hallelujah!

If you are like David, the shepherd boy, and look *up* and look *around*, you can confirm the general revelation or existence of God—the moon, the stars, the sun, the galaxy, the universe at large. You can't help but believe what the psalmist said— what is man that God is even mindful of him or pays attention to him.

Chapter 2

My Seven Years as an ABC Ministry Prayer Volunteer

*W*ell, I was selected in September 1997 by the prayer department to become one of the volunteer prayer partners. The individual who hired me was there at the *very* beginning of his ministry. I had a chance to go to his office and chat with him. We talked about a number of things, such as how the ministry got started and what was expected of me as a volunteer prayer partner. This was a *mega* ministry, and I was given a lot of leeway as a volunteer prayer partner. Since I was not on payroll, I had a regular job. I could come and go as I pleased.

I chose to work as a prayer partner volunteer over the weekend, especially on Saturday. The room held over a hundred people. I would come in, be seated, turn my phone on, and commence to answer phone calls for six solid hours.

What amazed me about many of the phone calls was the people struggling with depression. It was *shocking* and astounding since they were Christians. They would tell me that this had been going on for years, not weeks, not days, but for years, and that they had seen a psychologist or psychiatrist. My heart truly went out to them. Some were actually confined to a psychiatric ward at a mental institution. I just knew one thing: they needed deliverance by the Lord Jesus Christ, period.

Today there seems to be a huge pattern of mental illness among the body of believers. There were a number of biblical characters who experienced depression, which, after careful and considerate study, I found to be quite interesting and intriguing, such Elijah, Job, David, etc. These were very godly men, yet they experienced depression.

What exactly is depression? According to Webster's dictionary, it's the disorder of the mind; the breaking down of the mind with a mental disorder or incapacitation. What are some of the ways to get out of depression? Meditate, pray, or think on God's word. Doctors want to give you antidepressant medications to help you come out of depression. What are some of the Bible passages or verses one can meditate or think on? For example, Isaiah 26:3 says, "Whose mind is stayed on the Lord is kept in perfect or absolute peace or harmony." Second Timothy 1:7 declares that God did not give *us* the spirit of fear but of power, love, and a sound mind! Philippians 2:5 says, "Let that mind which was in Christ Jesus also be in you." Whatsoever things are true, pure, honest, lovely, of good report; think on these (Phil. 4:6–8). Our warfare is not carnal or fleshy but mighty through God in the pulling of vain imagination that tries to pull down strongholds and brings evil or wicked thought into obedience to our Lord and Savior Jesus Christ (2 Cor 10:4–5).

We must learn to recognize the works of the enemy and deal with them. The Bible declares that the god of this age has blinded the people to the saving knowledge of our Lord and savior Jesus Christ. For us to fight this, we must continue to declare the good news, no matter what it costs.

Since we are spiritual beings in physical bodies, our adversary, Satan, and his demons are spiritual beings who will use spiritual weapons to tear down the kingdom of God. That is why the apostle Paul is telling us our weapons are not carnal or fleshy (2 Cor. 10: 4–5) but spiritual to topple the enemy's onslaught (Eph. 6:10–18). Jesus combated the devil with the word of God (Matt. 4:4) to guarantee the victory. What a relationship. What insight! What discernment! God does not want us as believers to be ignorant of the devil's devices or strategies or tactics but be aware and very careful; the devil is very crafty! "Cast all your anxiety on him because he cares for you. Be alert and of sober mind. Your enemy the devil prowls around like a roaring lion looking for someone to devour" (1 Peter 5:7–8). We cannot thank the Godhead enough for its liberation or emancipation power. Hallelujah!

With these many, many believers and nonbelievers alike struggling with their spirituality, we need the liberation and emancipation power of the God of Abraham, Isaac, and Jacob to be unleashed against the power of darkness (Matt. 16:18). The Bible declares that God will build his church and the gates of hell shall not prevail. Hallelujah!

Since I have become a prayer partner, the enemy has intensified his attack against me on a personal level. It is not time to have a pity party but redouble my effort to become an overcomer! From the very beginning of time, the enemy has been subtle and crafty, starting with Adam and Eve in the garden of Eden, and humankind has been caught off guard and unprepared ever since—until the arrival of Jesus with his divine intervention.

As a volunteer prayer partner, God has put me here for a divine purpose to cast down vain imaginations, strongholds, and hindrance spirits. "We demolish arguments and every pretension that sets itself up against the knowledge of God, and we take captive every thought to make it obedient to Christ" (2 Cor. 10:5). It is indeed an honor and privilege to perform my duties faithfully. Hallelujah! God is our all in all, nothing less and nothing more.

Let me say this as a seasoned or veteran prayer partner: unless the Lord has literally called and ordained and anointed you to be a prayer partner, you will have a difficult time doing it because this is a ministry, not a mere job. People's lives are literally at stake. Please be aware!

During my seven years as a volunteer prayer partner, I had no trouble interacting with the people on the lines. It's amazing how people respond to authentic love, not counterfeit or pseudo love.

This chapter in my life came to a halt as a volunteer prayer partner on July 5, 2005. That is when I ceased to be a mere volunteer prayer partner and become a part of the regular staff, and this kicked my life up a notch.

Chapter 3

My Eight Years as an ABC Ministries Staff Member Prayer Partner

After being a volunteer for seven long years as an ABC prayer partner, I was officially hired on June 5, 2005, to be an ABC ministries prayer partner. It was not easy! There were fiery darts everywhere that tried to keep me from being hired. After I got a letter of recommendation from my pastor and they verified all of my references, I was finally let into the door, and I have been here ever since. What a privilege and honor to be allowed to pray for so many hurting people! When I was first hired, the wages were eight dollars an hour but are currently twelve dollars per hour, a whopping 50 percent increase without benefits. I thank the God of Abraham, Isaac, and Jacob for my position as a prayer partner. It has caused me to be the person I am today.

In my eight years as an ABC ministries prayer partner, we always under intensified spiritual warfare. The Bible, in Ephesians 6:10–14, says to put on the *whole armor* of God in order to contend with our adversary, the devil; well, what exactly is the armor of God? It is comprised of six components: the *belt* of *truth* (I am the way, the life, the truth, John 14:6); *breast* plate of *righteousness* (I am the righteousness of God, 2 Cor. 5:21); our feet shod with the preparation of the gospel of peace or good news (Eph. 6:15, Matt. 4:23); the *shield of faith* with which you will be able to quench or put all the fiery darts out of the evil one (1 Thess. 5:8); and take up the helmet of salvation (head gear, mind deliverance) (Eph. 6:17).

Last we have the sword of the spirit (Hebrews 4:12), the only offensive weapon. The previous five weapons were for defensive, not offensive purposes. You see, in Matthew 4:4 Jesus did not use the rudiments of philosophy or empty words to defend himself but God's word. The devil is well versed in God's word, so you need to be well versed by studying God's word to literally show yourself approved by God! That is why we as believers or Christians should take not only the time but also the energy to read and meditate upon the word of *God*!

As an ABC ministries prayer partner, you learn very quickly to categorize your phone calls. Perhaps the top five categories are marriage, finances, healing, health, and prosperity.

There would not be a day when people would not call about their *marriage*; the biggest complaint was adultery or infidelity on the behalf of the husband or wife. As prayer partners, we are not to counsel but to pray. There were two scriptures that I would pray: Malachi 2:16 and of course, Jeremiah 29:11. Malachi 2:16 talks about the wife of your youth and not to deal with her treacherously or deceitfully. In other words, do not be unfaithful to her; this will lead to disaster. If you maintain your vows and keep them, you will produce godly offspring, and this will, of course, please God. A person in the Bible who primarily accomplished this was named Abraham. Abraham produced Isaac and Isaac produced Jacob and Jacob produced Joseph, etc. The marriage is a covenant institution produced by God himself. You see, when a man and a woman marry, they enter a covenant between each other and God. Hallelujah! What is covenant? It is a contract, agreement, or pact with each other.

God commenced from the beginning with Adam, which was called the Adamic covenant. Covenants are what we do not pay much attention to today; covenants are made and broken each and every day. Take, for example, marriage. Many people do not see marriage as a covenant, and that is why it is so easily broken. Therefore, we have a 50 percent divorce rate; one out of every two couples is divorced. To me that is a shame. There simply is not any difference between the church and the world as far as the attitude about divorce. We are not taking God's word seriously. God hates divorce!

It is all about obeying God's word in order to reap God's benefits. We can't just select what we want to do and leave the rest. It does not work that way. The Bible declares it is better to obey than to sacrifice (1 Samuel 15:22). God is interested in obedience rather than sacrifice!

After *marriage*, the next thing we categorize is *finances*. People would call and tell us they needed finances. Somehow or another, they were not prospering in their finances; they were paying their tithes and giving their offerings but were not prospering. Go figure. I would pray Matthew 6:33, "But first seek the kingdom of God and his righteousness." If you do, all these things will be added to you. That was my answer to their problem or rather God's answer to their problem. In addition, I would take them to Jeremiah 29:11. I know my thoughts toward you are peace and not evil. I plan to bless, so you may have a future. If you are going through a financial crisis, remember God and his trustworthy word. Too many times we want a formula or method, and that is putting God in a box, so to speak. We can't do that. God is first and foremost not a formula or method but a vast, intelligent supernatural being who has endless ways of meeting our most basic and fundamental needs. Just keep paying your tithes and giving your offerings (Mal. 3:10). Watch how God works for you, his child. Yes, there are hardships for believers. Paul told Timothy we will suffer hardship, but we must endure as God's soldiers in the army of the Lord. No one said that our journey as believers would be a "piece of cake" or "a trip through the tulips"; far from it. We as believers must always fight the good fight of faith. Endure hardship; it comes with the territory (1 Tim. 6:12)!

The third category was *health*. This is probably among the greatest need in the body of Christ—good health. "I pray that you may prosper in *all* things and be in *health*, just as your soul prospers" (3 John 2). Regardless of how great our marriage and finances may be going, without good health, it could prove counterproductive or *un*fruitful. We need our bodies to be in the proper working order. Jesus declared in John 10:10, "I come that you may have life more abundantly or bountifully". In other words, Jesus wants us to prosper in our health so we can enjoy life a whole lot better.

And even another category is *healing*. When your marriage and finances are going great and all of a sudden illness or infirmity pops up, now you are in store for a *healing*. Where do I go from here? Frankly, you gird up your loins and go to the Lord in prayer. For example, pray Isaiah 53:4–5, James 5:16, and 1 Peter 2:24, and before you know it, you will have experienced a full recovery! Thank the Lord for His healing by the grace of God! Hallelujah. Praise the Lord. The best is yet to come!

Whenever people think of the word *prosperity,* the majority think it's about money. Well, let me tell you what Webster says about prosperity. It means to succeed at whatever you're doing. In the Old Testament in the book of Genesis, a man named Joseph did exactly that. The Bible said he would prosper wherever he went and God was with him. Joseph was a prototype Christ. He lived an impeccable life and of course, did not did save his family and perhaps the rest of the world too! Praise the Lord!

Chapter 4

They Were Blessed as
They Went! Hallelujah!

Blessed: favor; fortunate; enviable; happy; praised; magnify; honor; glorify; sanctified. "The *just* shall live by *faith*" (Hab. 2:4). Just: righteous; honorable; pious; sacred; devout; virtuous; holy. Faith: trust; confidence; credence; conviction; assurance; certainty. We walk by faith and not by sight (2 Cor 5:7)! Trust or faith is the matter or *substance* of things desired, *hoped* for, and the proof or *evidence* of things not seen (Heb. 11:1)! Without belief or faith it is impossible to please God (Heb 11:6)! Faith (belief) comes by hearing, listening and hearing by the word (*rhema*) of God (Romans 10:17), being consistent in applying all the steps needed to achieve your goals with success.

First and foremost, we as believers must develop our ability to *walk* or *live* by *faith* and not by *sight*! In my work as a prayer partner at ABC ministries, I get so many calls from callers who do not have a clue as to what it is to walk by faith, not by sight! These are not what we call baby believers but older believers in the faith who are still being spoon fed! They have failed to read their Bibles, search the scriptures, and evaluate what they are hearing and experiencing! They were blessed as they went! Like anything you do in life, you must exercise or apply it! However, if you fail to apply or exercise your faith, it will become weak and feeble, and therefore, you will suffer atrophy—the weakening of your potential spiritual muscle! You need to get busy by exercising your spiritual faith on a day-by-day basis! It simply takes one day at a time. Inch by inch is a cinch. How does one make a thousand-mile journey? One step at a time. What do I mean when I say that they (believers) were blessed as they (believers) went? That is why it's essential that we read our Bible, both *Old* and *New* Testament! It is wonderful to have a working knowledge of both the Old (Hebrew) and New (Greek) Testament. Without reading the Old Testament, you will not be equipped or prepared to understand the New Testament! Take, for example, Genesis 3:15, which is the first messianic prediction about the seed of the *woman* and the *serpent*. It declares that the seed of the serpent shall bruise the heel of the seed of woman, and her seed crushing the head of the serpent simply speaks about Jesus's death, burial, and resurrection, destroying the devil at Calvary. After Calvary, it's a done deal. John 19:30 declares it's finished. And according to Romans 16:20, the God of peace shall bruise Satan under your feet shortly.

The Bible is so essential in telling us what God's will is for us. The will of God is contained within the pages of the Bible. He declares that the just shall live by faith (Habakkuk 2:4). As I began to reflect upon the people in the Bible who were blessed as they went in scripture, I could not help but reflect upon Abram, who eventually became Abraham, the father of many nations. Abraham was simply chosen by God unilaterally, and that was that. What an amazing thing. The God of this universe reached down through the portal of time and chose Abraham out of eternity. What a shock. Abraham came from the Middle East, I believe modern-day Iraq of the land of Chaldean or Babylon. My take on this is he was supposedly a moon worshiper before encountering Jehovah, the self-existing God. After God revealed himself to Abraham, Abraham was a changed man. Abraham's original name was Abram, father of faith, later, father of the multitude, and one thing led to another. Abram had a wife named Sarai, who happened to be beautiful and barren. Her barrenness proved to be a reproach upon her. Abram by now was called Abraham, and Sarai Sarah; both names had been changed by Jehovah, the self-existing God, for the express purpose of letting everyone know that there had been some changes made around there and this was supposed to reflect how they lived.

Abraham and Sarah, his wife, were blessed as they went. Abraham had a servant named Eleazer. He was the only heir because of Sarah's barrenness, but God moved right (in) and changed all of that. Jehovah did this by promising an heir to both Abraham and Sarah. At the ages of seventy-five and sixty-five, they both were promised by God that they would have a son to be their heir to their estate. In the intervening years, since they had not conceived a son naturally, they came up with the idea of a surrogate mom by the name of Hagar. As a result of this, a son named Ismael was produced, which led to all kinds of repercussions, namely Hagar being kicked out of the household after Isaac was born and banished to the wilderness, where Jehovah came to Hagar's rescue and promised that her son would produce many nations of royalty. To me, God blessed Hagar in spite of herself. Hagar and Ismael were not a part of the original or primary plan; God blessed them as they went.

After all, God told *Abram* and *Sarai* to move from one location unto another. Abram and Sarai were told by God to be *patient*, as one of the incentives to receive the blessings of God as they were making their journey of faith. This would not be easy. Since Abraham and Sarah were constantly on the move, they simply were tent dwellers. As Abraham and Sarah were making their way to the Promised Land by way of the wilderness, things got better and better as they went.

I used the patriarch of the Bible to illustrate my point of being blessed as they went: Abraham, Isaac, and Jacob were perfect examples of how God blessed them in so many, many ways as they journey to the Promised Land. They amassed great fortunes and wealth because of the blessings of Jehovah, the self-existing God.

There were many times when I was blessed as I went! For example, my car ran out of gas on numerous occasions, and I was always able to get gas money from relatives, friends, acquaintances, etc. God always had a ram in the bush. This was God's way of blessing me. Also, there were times when I could not pay my bills, but my God supplied my most primary and fundamental needs. An unexpected check from Uncle Sam—hallelujah! Praise the Lord! We are acutely aware that we are people who live by faith and walk by faith and not by sight. Praise the Lord! Our spiritual forefather knew how to walk by faith!

As believers, we must continue to persevere on our spiritual journey, which gives us the spiritual guts to keep on going when there is nothing. Go again! Hallelujah! Praise the Lord! As we go on our way we share our faith with others to propagate the gospel, we are blessed as we go. Thank you, Jesus! The just shall live by faith, and not by sight. It is very essential that we stay on fire for God to give ourselves a boost of this hope that lies deep within us as genuine believers of the good news. God has equipped us already to do exceedingly good works to advance the kingdom of God. He commissioned us to go into the world and share this good news with others. By sharing this good news, we as believers will be blessed in so many, many ways! God promised in His holy word that He would meet our most primary, fundamental, and basic needs, but we must always, according to Matthew 6:33, first seek the kingdom of God and God's righteousness, have a right standing with Jehovah, and all of these things would be added to us. The God we serve is not only a wonderful God, but He is also a marvelous God. He is a God of excellence, worthy to be praised and glorified. Hallelujah! Thank you, Jesus, for saving me from a lost eternity and ultimately damnation without remedy!

As I said at the outset, we as genuine believers are commissioned to walk by faith and not by sight; we are blessed as we go. In other words, nothing happens unless we are motivated to live by faith. That is the motivating factor in doing what we do. We, as believers, do not have to rely on our own personal limited resources or finite resource, but we are to look to Jehovah Jireh, the self-existing God, with unlimited resources at each believer's disposal. Hallelujah; praise the Lord, and thank you, Jesus!

Chapter 5

The Best Is Yet to Come!

In Jeremiah 29:11, Jeremiah was called to the nations as a prophet before he was born, yet in his mother's womb. What a revelation by God (Jeremiah 1:5)! The strange thing about Jeremiah's calling as a prophet to nations and kingdoms was his unwillingness to obey. After all, he was but a youth! Moses did exactly the same thing, but God yet used him mightily. Yes, there were men unwilling to be used by God; yes, Jeremiah was one of them. Jeremiah allowed his phobias to influence his thinking, but Jehovah (God) did not stand idly and allow Jeremiah to think like this but challenged him to think and do differently. Jehovah explained to Jeremiah that as a prophet to the nations and kingdoms, he would speak through Jeremiah to these people and not to be afraid but to be bold and courageous in front of these people and tell them, "Thus said the Lord." Jeremiah was known as the weeping prophet because he was so sensitive and compassionate toward God's people, who eventually turned on him and persecuted him because of his message of doom and gloom. Things did not look very good for Jeremiah. They were so caught in sin that their consciences became seared. Sin had so impacted the people that they were not sensitive to the prompting of the Holy Spirit. That explains why the people of God were rejecting Jehovah's convicting them of their sin of idolatry. They had sinned so much that their hearts became very hardened, thus making it difficult for them to be convicted. They actually loved their sins, which, of course, was not good.

Solomon had kept the northern and southern kingdoms united for many, many years during his lifetime because of his lifestyle, which led the united kingdom into idolatry. Well, after Solomon's death and because of his son, the united kingdom became divided. Israel became the northern kingdom (ten) tribes; Judah became the southern kingdom (two) tribes (Dan; Benjamin). No matter how you looked at it, idolatry was the culprit! For so many, many years, Solomon kept the kingdom united under his rulership or leadership because of his alliances through marriages with so many women over the years. These were strange women who had their own gods, and thus idolatry was running rampant under Solomon's rulership.

Before the splitting or breakup of the united kingdom into a divided kingdom, one to the *north* (Israel) one to the *south* (Judah), both were involved in idolatry. This certainly was not pleasing to God. The southern kingdom perhaps had the better kings as opposed to the northern kingdom, which had wicked ones. You would frequently read about the divided kingdom and what was going on with the kings, especially the northern kingdom kings. They were mostly evil and wicked and did not follow God. They did things to suit themselves, which was disastrous and of course, tragic!

Well anyway, God simply got fed up with these not only wicked kings but also wicked people who were very steeped in idolatry. So God raised up the wicked nation of Assyria to destroy the northern kingdom and exile the people. The *purpose* or *reason* that God raised up the Assyrians to destroy Israel was that God was tired of Israel's failure to repent and get right with God. This is sort of an irony—God using a wicked gentile nation to destroy a Jewish nation because of idolatry! The vicious or barbaric Assyrian army not only attacked and mauled Israel but took some into captivity. The Assyrians were very fierce and cruel people who loved to torment their captives and terrify them. The Assyrians' reputation preceded them to the point that many Israelites committed suicide rather than submit to physical and emotional abuse by the Assyrians because the Assyrians were very thorough and painstaking in their ability to torture one! God achieved his objective through the

Assyrians' powerful military. The Assyrians did a thorough job of ransacking Israel. The northern kingdom made the false assumption that God wouldn't punish them for their spiritual adultery or infidelity or unfaithfulness. They acknowledged God with their lips but forsook him with their hearts. They had a form of godliness but denied the power thereof, so we must be careful that we are indeed walking with God as Enoch had done by faith. We need to examine or take stock of ourselves to see if we are still in the faith. We can subtly find ourselves drifting or straying from the pillar of faith. Are you witnessing? Are you testifying? Are you fellowshipping? Are you devoting time to prayer? These things will help keep on the straight and narrow path and not allow you to drift onto the broad path. Stay on your knees quite frequently and this will ensure a life above reproach or scandal.

Look at, for example, Billy Graham's life over sixty years of ministry. There was never a scandal because of Billy's Graham's consistent accountability and integrity before the Lord. Not only was there no scandal within Graham's ministry, but the same held true for Billy's son, Franklin Graham. The checks and balances kept these things possible with great prayer partners to undergird the overall ministry. Hallelujah!

Weeping may endure for a night, but joy comes in the morning (Psalm 30:4)! In other words, no matter what you are going through, there is always a silver lining or light at the end of the tunnel. To God be the glory! Yes! The book of Jeremiah written by Jeremiah speaks about doom, gloom, melancholy, and many, many things that were not very encouraging. As a matter of fact, it could be downright discouraging. Jeremiah was only doing what the Lord said, Anyway, getting back to Jeremiah 29:11: "For I know the thoughts that I think toward you, says the Lord; thoughts of *peace* and not of *evil*, to give you a *future* and a *hope*." This is the scripture I utilize to encourage believers who are struggling with their Christian faith. Jehovah God is telling them his thoughts toward them are not evil but peace and hope with an expected end; in other words, a bright and sunny future! Praise Jehovah God for that rhema word!

The Lord spoke these very encouraging, inspirational, and motivational words to Jeremiah to let him know that he had a *purpose* and *plan* for his people after seventy years in exile in Babylon, and it was high time for them to celebrate their coming home! Now since that three score and ten mandate of exile was officially over, Jehovah's people were now permitted to return to their native land and continue to resume their lives. Hallelujah! During these seventy years of captivity, Jehovah God had a remnant.

Although God's people had virtually given themselves over to idolatry, God had a ram in the bush; in other words, God had a remnant—those who would intercede for those who had gone into exile captivity for three score and ten years.

Many people ask why Jehovah God utilized a gentile nation to punish Judah for her sin of idolatry. This gentile nation was guilty of the same thing, but God utilized this gentile nation to bring punishment to all of us we don't know. Since God is sovereign and infinite and we are not, we leave all of these things to him. All I know is Romans 8:28 declares we know all things work together for good to them that love God and are called according to His purpose.

Many, many things had to happen to Jehovah's or God's people before they could reap the benefits and blessings of God's divine favor. It just didn't happen automatically! They had to go through something in spite of their disobedience. Once again, after hearing the negative caller, I presented the antidote to the caller of Jeremiah 29:11; the best is yet to come no matter what your situation is. God declares, "I will build my church, and the gates of hell will not prevail against it" (Matt. 16:18)! Praise Jehovah or God! Well, my journey through the fifth chapter concerning Jeremiah 29:11 has come to a conclusion of God's, Jehovah's, Elohim's, Elelyon's best for his people!

Chapter 6

Why I Never Quit!

What does it mean to quit? According to Webster's dictionary, to quit simply means to: depart from; to leave; to cease from; to give up; to let go; to stop doing a thing; to discourage; to renounce; to surrender. Quitter: goldbrick dropout; shirker; slacker. Quitter: piker; deserter; gives up easily without trying; to forsake; to abandon; to depart. (Scriptures: Deut. 32:15; Job 1:5; Josh. 1:5; Deut. 7:24; 2 Chron. 12:1 page 55 NASB; 2 Chron. 15:2; Ezra 9:9, God has not forsaken!; Jer. 5:7; Heb. 13:5. Depart: never knew you, Matt. 7:23.)

First and foremost, this is a basic, primary, fundamental philosophy universally: winners never, ever quit; losers never, ever win! As a man thinks, so is he. If you think like a loser, you will behave like a loser. Simple as that! The biggest reason I never, ever quit was my family, especially on my mother's side. They were staunch believers, from mom's mom, Lee Joe, to my mom, Algerine Joe. We truly loved God. Simple as that!

Even before I took a fifteen-year hiatus from God's influence in my personal life, I was exposed to the gospel before I knew what it was as a young child attending church regularly. Believe it or not, you learn more by catching rather than someone telling you something. When it came to Christianity, I learned more by observation than verbal communication. People can talk all they want, but are they living it?

Since my mom was the most educated academically in our household when it came to parenting, I had the tendency to gravitate toward her for parenting instruction, and it worked out rather well. As I was growing up, I noticed that my mom, Algerine, was always reading the Holy Bible—literally every day. I never gave it any serious thought until years later. Mom always took us to church with her, thank God. In our household, our mom was the spiritual leader, as simple as that. Our dad, however, was not inclined to be our spiritual leader. He had issues that only could be addressed by God himself, which would take place years into the future. As I reflect back upon my personal life as the child of a believer, I became more thankful and grateful that God permitted me to be born into such a household. In addition, I was born into one of the most powerful countries in the world: the United States of America. Hallelujah!

My mother as a Christian was very steadfast and unmovable over the years. She was very focused in her relationship with Jesus Christ, without a doubt. She did not allow anyone or anything to distract her, so you can imagine why I never quit my Christian faith over the years. My mother was the initial driving force behind my faith up until she passed away. After that, it was strictly Jesus Christ and me. Don't get me wrong, I always was a believer in Jesus Christ from the time I was thirty-two until now and don't plan on quitting anytime soon. We as believers must have a sound and solid confidence in Jesus Christ as our personal Lord and Savior, because if you don't, you could wind up drifting away.

The reason I never quit as a genuine believer was because it was never an option. As a youth when I took a hiatus or leave from the things of God, it was because of my sheer ignorance and not being a genuine believer because of lack of knowledge. As a youth, you only know so much, and that is it. Even though I left off attending church for fifteen years, God kept a steady hand on my life. That's the only way I can explain it. When I ceased attending church and started partying, drinking, and hanging out, this is when I detected that this God had an investment in me. For example, I got drafted at twenty years of age and should have gone straight to Vietnam, where about 90 percent of young men went; but God had other plans, thanks to a praying mom who not only prayed but kicked in a little fasting to boot. It was just amazing how God (Jehovah) was working things out behind the invisible scenes, and the same held true for my brother, Perry Jr. We both are army veterans and both are serving the Lord because of a praying mom.

There is absolutely no substitute for a praying mom. My mom never did give up on me or quit on me. She was not a slacker but a steadfast, unmovable, unshakable believer who stayed and finished the course and left a huge legacy behind for her family—King Jesus!

I firmly believe in Philippians 1:6, which declares, "For I am confident or assured of this very thing, that he, Jehovah, who began a good work *in* you will perfect or complete it until the day of Jesus Christ!" This means his imminent return. Praise the Lord, anyhow! And of course, another profound truth that comes out of Hebrews 13:5–6 is that Jehovah will never leave you nor forsake you. We may boldly declare or say that the Lord is my helper. I will not fear what man can do to me. Hallelujah—praise the Lord! Thank you, Jesus. In addition to Hebrews 13:5–6 is Hebrews 12:1: "Therefore, since we have so great a cloud of witnesses surrounding us, let us also lay aside every encumbrance (burden) and the *sin* which so easily entangles (traps; ensnares) us, and let us run with endurance (patient) the race that is set before us!"

Since what we as believers are doing is not about *us,* but it's about Jesus, we must love *him*. Therefore, our focus must be on King Jesus. It's once again not about *us* but *him*; first seek the kingdom of God and his righteousness and all of these things will be added unto us. It just does not take that much to be a quitter, a loser, a goldbrick, or a slacker or to simply drop out of the race. Remember that this is a race; be careful what kind of race you're in: the fifty meters, one hundred meters, or twenty-six kilometers (miles). Gear up and count the cost!

Chapter 7

The Fruit of the Spirit!

Galatians 5:21–22 refers to fruit: produce such as berry, apple, orange, pear, grain, nut, plum, grapefruit, citron, banana, pineapple, etc., edible produce of the earth for man's consumption! These are the consequences of our conduct or the qualities possessed by Christians. Metaphor: good/bad conduct.

As a believer in Jesus, I feel that we should *cultivate* or *develop* the fruit of the spirit. It would enhance us greatly in our walk with God Jehovah on a daily basis. Since God (Jehovah) is love (1 John 4:8), we as believers should be about love (compassion, devotion, commitment). Jesus was quoted as saying the world would know Christians by the love that they would have one for another (John 13:35). *What* a revelation, an insight, a disclosure, a word. Oftentimes this is not the case! I truly don't know why! Could it be a *cultural* thing, a *race* thing, or a matter of the *heart*? All of these things can be very problematic if we fail to yield to the Holy Spirit. We must learn to walk in the spirit, not the flesh! No matter who we are, we certainty must definitely work on this situation if we are to be set free, delivered, released, liberated, and emancipated from these very devastating tendencies, habits, and proclivities. We must literally learn to die to self! Ouch!

Predicated or *based* upon personal observation in America, the church is not very progressive when it comes to the mixing or blending of the races or integration. It is almost like it's taboo or forbidden. We have to let go, let God! When it comes to being progressive, the world is way ahead of the church. You ask, "Why? Is it a double standard? Is it a cultural thing?" If this is the case, we need God's help in changing! The very *purpose* for the church being in the world but not of it (world) is to impact in the same way as the first-century church turned theirs upside down—what an impact!

The sad commentary is the world is impacting the church in an adverse way, which ought not be! Culture has crept into the church instead the church creeping into the culture! The primary reason, I believe, the modern church has not impacted the world is that it has lost its *salt*—that is, its influence—and became like the world. In other words, it blended in! That is not good. We as the church must maintain our uniqueness or light period!

So what made the first-century believers *so* different than the twenty-first-century believers? First and foremost, the ancient church was not far removed from Jesus's ascension. It was still fresh. They were literally eyewitnesses and could testify about it! They had the fire in their *bellies*. The fruit of the Spirit was alive and well. The apostle Paul had yet to come along until around the ninth chapter of Acts. It was a glorious time and still fresh. The Bible declares Jesus is the same yester*day*, to*day*, and for*ever*. Therefore, we ought to be able to turn our world upside down, too. What's the secret? Walking in the Spirit! The same Holy Spirit is present today as he was back then. Far too many Christians are not walking in the Spirit today. Most Christians are like the church at Corinthians. They are too far carnal and not enough spiritual, and of course this weighs very heavily on the body of Christ. As a result, the world is left unchanged. Paul made it perfectly clear that in the Christian experience, love is the key/operative word. If it is not done in love, what is the point? Love is something everyone can use or experience. If you have been taught the proper way to love, you can be invaluable.

Upon careful examination of the fruit of the spirit in Galatians 5:22, we find it begins with the word *love*, and everything else flows from love, like: joy, peace, patience, kindness, goodness, faithfulness, gentleness, and self-control. Against such things there is no law! The Paraclete comforter, the Holy Spirit, was sent to help (helper). Since God's very nature, attribute, character, and essence is love, from there flows everything else. The Bible declares in 1 John 4:8, "*God is love!*" Need I say any more? Since God is love, we can't lose. As the scriptures say, if we walk in the Spirit, we will not fulfill the lust of the flesh. If we stay in the love of God (Jehovah), we will be just fine. The Paraclete will help us do God's will, plan, or purpose. It's amazing what can be done through obedience.

The reason I entitled chapter 7 "The Fruit of the Spirit" was because any genuine work you do for God has to be Spirit induced, not flesh induced! It won't count if done in the energy of the flesh. Godly induced work is highly approved. No matter how long or short a time one has been walking with the Lord, we always need his precious Holy Spirit to lead, guide, advise, direct, and counsel us! The Bible declares that the righteous will be led by the spirit! Notice I didn't say the (fruits) of the Spirit but the fruit—singular, not plural. It is very important that we know this. There is one Spirit with many, many different fruits (Gal. 5:22). "Love" and "God"—love means agape love. In John 3:16, it says, "For God *so* loved the world ..."

Joy means gladness, cheerfulness, liveliness, ecstasy. The joy of the Lord is my strength (Neh. 8:10).

Peace means calmness, tranquility, serenity, absent of conflict. Isaiah 26:3 says, "You will keep in perfect or complete peace, whose mind is stayed on you! Because he trusts in you!"

Patience means perseverance, persistence, suffering (trials), calm endurance, endure it with patience (1 Pet. 2:20).

Kindness means tenderness, compassion, consideration, and understanding. Micah 6:8 says, "O Man, what is good, and what does the Lord require of you, but to do justice, to love kindness, and walk humbly with your God."

Goodness means excellence, value, and virtue. Psalm 23:6 says, "Surely goodness and mercy will follow you all the days of your life."

Faithfulness means loyalty, dependability, and fidelity. Deuteronomy 32:4 says God is a God of faithfulness. God can't fail. He's always faithful!

Gentleness means kindness, tenderness, softness, delicacy, and sweetness. There is a spirit of gentleness among believers (1 Cor. 4:21).

Self-control means reserve, restraint, self-discipline, balance, and discrete. We as God's (Jehovah's) children must allow the fruit of the Spirit to rule our lives.

Without the fruit of the Spirit playing a vital and significant part in the believer's life, his or her life will not impact nonbelievers' lives as much! Paul in the fifth chapter of Galatians knew what he was talking about to be content in all things. What separates the Christian faith from all faith is the relationship with Jesus Christ. Jesus Christ is the deciding factor in it all. No matter where one comes from, Jesus Christ is able to separate the good from evil. Faith in the Lord Jesus Christ has yet to steer anyone in the wrong direction, no matter what race you are, what culture you are, or where you are from. God gives us the Holy Spirit at redemption—hallelujah! The fruit of the Spirit is uniquely a God thing, not a man thing. No matter what man does, he cannot replicate what only God can do through the Holy Spirit: the love, the joy, the peace, the patience, the kindness, the goodness, the faithfulness, the gentleness, and the self-control.

After much observation, evaluation, and assessment, we have come up with the final analysis that without John 15:5, you cannot do anything. It is a God thing to have a good relationship with Jesus Christ. One must have a born-again experience with Jesus Christ.

Chapter 8

There Is Faith, Hope, and Charity!
The Greatest Is Love or Charity!

First Corinthians 13:13 talks about faith, hope, and charity.

Faith means complete trust, confidence, assurance, conviction, fidelity, and certainty.

Hope means reliance upon the future, count on, rely.

Charity means benevolence, kindness, and commission.

When Paul wrote 1 Corinthians 13:13, the church was having some issues at the seaport and very decadent city called Corinthians. It took at least two letters before the *mission* was completed. We as believers and especially as prayer (partners) must always walk by faith and not by sight! Second Corinthians 5:7 says the just shall live by faith. Habakkuk 2:4 says, "See, the enemy is puffed up; his desires are not upright—but the righteous person will live by his faithfulness." Just because you wake up each day, don't put your life on auto.

As believers and especially prayer partners, we must wake up excited about each and every day's spiritual potential. Don't allow life to become *mundane, routine, a drag,* or *a bore*; get up full of faith and excitement and enthusiasm and devote some time to Jehovah God and let him know what's on your heart and mind. As long as we are in these earth suits called bodies, we have to exercise our Jehovah God–given measure of faith. God has given us a measure of faith. Romans 12:3 says, "For by the grace given me I say to every one of you: Do not think of yourself more highly than you ought, but rather think of yourself with sober judgment, in accordance with the faith God has distributed to each of you." The idea behind this concept is to separate from our Lord and Savior Jesus Christ, who had faith without measure. However, we believers are limited by our measure of faith, that which the Lord has granted to us. But God is not limited! That is why God is the God of the impossibilities. Don't put yourself or God into an itty-bitty, tiny box. God is liable to break out of the box.

Faith is very, very pivotal in our walk with the Lord. On one occasion Jesus's disciples had trouble casting out a devil in a young boy because of the *littleness* of their faith, which was quite puzzling to them. Then Jesus said something unusual: "Truly I say to you, if you had the faith of a grain of mustard seed, you can move mountains" (Matthew 17:20). As long as we occupy these physical, terrestrial, earthly bodies, we certainly will need our faith. Without faith it is impossible to please God. Once again, the just shall by faith. Jehovah God designed or set it up this way. Even in Genesis God called Abram out of the land of Chaldea to strictly follow him and changed his name from Abram, "called of God," to Abraham, "father of the multitude," without giving him any advance instruction to go by. He went by faith. This is what separated Abraham from all the rest. He simply believed God and soon followed him. We need our faith as Abraham needed his faith to do the things he did. According to Romans 4:17, "We call those things that be not as though they already were." Genesis 17:6 says, "I will make thee exceeding fruitful, and will make nations of thee, and kings shall come of thee!"

The word *faith* is simply a word, but when you attach the dynamics to it, release into the atmosphere of prayer, things begin to happen. It sets off a chain reaction, and things start to occur, which is good! Until Jehovah God brings this world to a close, as we know for believers as well as nonbelievers, things will continue to be a bit confusing and of course, uncertain. Why would God utilize this method or system to aid and assist man in his journey heavenward? You can't taste heaven (faith); you can't feel faith; and you can't see faith, yet it plays a vital and significant role in our daily lives. Once again, according to Hebrews 11:1: "Now faith is the *substance* (matter, material, being, object, element) of things *hoped* (lean on, depend on, count on, look forward to) *for*, the *evidence* (proof, data, testimony, confirmation, manifestation, apparent, visible, obvious)." Jehovah (self-existing) God mentioned in Hebrews 11:3 that through this unique word called *faith*, we *comprehend* or *grasp* or understand that the *worlds* (the universe, humankind, people generally, the public, planets, creation nature) were *framed* (to make, to construct, to erect, to build) by the *word*. The word was in the beginning, and the word was God. *Logos*—the word was with God! John 1:1 says, "So that things which are seen were not made of things (objects, items) which do appear" (Ps. 33: 6, 9).

The Bible declares that it is impossible to please God without faith (Heb. 11:6). In other words, one must believe who he says he is. Thank God for holy scriptures to prove or confirm his holy word. Once again, the believer's experience must *line* up with the word of God! In order to confirm or prove or substantiate without a shadow of doubt, Jehovah's word must be confirmed by holy scripture. No doubt about it, period!

As we close out chapter 8 concerning the big three, faith, hope, and charity, the greatest of the big three is charity, which is an old English word for *love*. God is love (1 John 4:16). This word *charity* is benevolence for charity organizations (giving). How can you not mention *faith* without mentioning the other! They all seem to *link* or *go* together. As long as we on this earth as genuine believers in this real Jesus, we must extend a helping hand of faith, hope, and charity.

According to the scriptures, God's very nature, attribute, character, traits, and essence is love. First John 4:16 describes God as love. Hallelujah. *Faith* is not one Jehovah's characteristics in the genuine sense of who he is. *Hope* is not one God's traits to describe!

Chapter 9

Not *My* Will Be Done,
but *Thy* Will Be Done (Luke 22:42)

What does the word *will* mean? Definition: according to Webster it means the power to do what one wants to do, an attitude, a purpose. Will: one's own volition, wish, desire, inclination, proclivity, tendency; to have power to make willful decisions based on one our volition (freedom to make choices). We have the freedom to make a choice/decision.

Jehovah God was very wise when he made humankind in his own image and gave to them a free will, therefore not making them robots or mechanical servants. Mine means it belongs to me. Thine means it belongs to you. Luke 22:42 shows Jesus battling or struggling with his will versus God's will. It was not an automatic thing or something you just do without thinking about it, especially when it comes to laying one's life down. Jehovah God knew in advance before the foundation of the world what *his plan, purpose,* and *will* were for *his* only begotten, preeminent Son. When Jesus's time came, it was only obvious, clear, and plain that, without doubt, he was to die on a rugged cross.

You may ask, "What does Jehovah God's will have to do with my own individual will? A *whole* lot!" To be frank and honest with you, we as believers must come to the conclusion that we have been bought or purchased with a price and that we are not our own. Hallelujah! Far too many saints have no problem with Jesus as Savior but are unwilling to submit to him as Lord. This can pose a deep problem for the saint. If Jesus is good enough to be Savior, certainly he is good enough to be Lord. We must recognize this once and for all, period.

We as believers, as we walk with the Lord, will find ourselves in situations or circumstances we had absolutely nothing to do with. Jehovah God is trying to demonstrate to his children how powerful and mighty he is, no question about it. There are only certain circumstances God can deliver you out of. As believers, it is never ever going to be easy. First Peter 5:8 says, "Our adversary, the devil, is like a roaring lion to seek whom he may devour. Resist (him) and he shall flee." Get ready. If you don't know it now, you never, ever will. We wrestle not with flesh and blood, but with spiritual wickedness in high places. As long as we believers know who our adversary is, we can properly wage war against him. People are truly gullible and do not readily read their Bibles constantly as they should. People act as though they need to be spoon-fed and get off of the meds to help eliminate such situations. As I declared early on, there is no such thing as a free walk through the tulips. Walk quietly but carry a big stick. Jehovah God's proclamation is, "We will build our church, and the gates of hell shall not prevail against it" (Matt. 16:18).

I have discovered during my Christian experiences whether or not to do my will or God's will. The choice is yours. No matter how you dice it, the choice is yours. Hallelujah! After all is said and done, of course, and after the smoke is cleared, and the dust settled, the bottom line is did you do the will of the Father? That is, of course, the point or crux of the matter.

Jesus once declared, "My sisters, brothers, mothers are the ones who do the will of my father. God! Jehovah!" (Mark 3:35). Here the issue or point was obeying God or doing Jehovah's will. The key in walking with God is doing his wonderful will regardless. In my one score and ten journey as a believer, I was, above all else, concerned about doing the will of God. This was my most primary, fundamental, and basic desire or priority because once you start to do God's will, everything else falls into line. Hallelujah! Praise Jesus!

How does one find the will of God for one's life?

By happenstance?

By luck?

By lot?

By fleece?

By accident?

No, it's by the word of God and by others speaking into your life God's word. The *key* to finding God's will for your life is found in God's world (word)—the holy Bible. For example; 2 Peter 3:9 says that it's not God's will that any should perish but all should come to repentance and be saved. Hallelujah! Because of the word of God, I became a follower of Jesus Christ. I heard 2 Corinthians 5:17 preached one day, which says that we walk by faith and not by sight. Faith comes by hearing and hearing by the word of God. Therefore, I trusted Jesus Christ as my personal Lord and Savior. Hallelujah! Romans 10:13 declares whosoever will call upon the Lord shall be saved.

We as saints of God must know the will of God for our lives from the holy scriptures. If we as saints of God do not place a premium on reading God's word, how else are we going to know God's will for our lives? As believers or saints, we are here to glorify God while we are on this earth. That's God's plan, purpose, and will for our lives respectively. We need to take stock of our lives and cast off the insignificant and hold onto the significant. Once again, it's about doing the will of God, not about doing your own thing or pursuing your own hidden agenda. It is about getting the job done individually or corporately. Hallelujah! Praise the Lord! Thank you, Jesus! The best is yet to come.

God has a clarion or a clear calling on each person's individual life. That is why one should, at an early age, find out one's gift. After becoming a believer thirty years ago, I discovered I had the gifts of both pastor and teacher by endeavoring both to pastor and to teach at small community churches. I taught a Bible study to learn more about God's word over the years, and in addition to that, I would go into the pulpit and preach sermons to the people to get their response, which was affirmative. These things provided proof that I had these qualities and gifts from God. Hallelujah! I have been doing them both for nearly three decades. Make sure of your calling from God by just doing it. The very reason I knew that I was called to both pastor and teach was because I did not pursue it or want it. To do these things was the last thing on my mind. I was called by God, not man.

Since I was called nearly three decades ago to both be a pastor and a teacher, I have gone on to both pastor a church in Los Angeles and teach as well. What a joy, what a privilege, what an honor to be called by God. These gifts are irrevocable according to God's word in Romans 11:29. What encouragement! What inspiration! What motivation! Praise God from whom all blessing flows. God has placed his mark upon me over the years. Since I have been called by God, I have to make my calling based upon the word of God a sure thing by equipping myself with proper tools: Bible, concordance, maps, etc. With much fear and trembling, I make my calling sure. Thank the Lord! Hallelujah!

Chapter 10

But First Seek Ye the Kingdom of God and His Righteousness and All These Things Will Be Added unto You (Matt. 6:33)

What exactly is the kingdom of God? Jesus was talking to his disciples about it, such as taking no thought about what shall we eat, drink, and wear. All of these things do the gentiles seek, and your heavenly father knows that you have need of all these things. Take therefore no thought for tomorrow, for tomorrow shall take thought for the things of itself. Hallelujah! Praise God! Thank you, Jesus!

Jesus is saying in all of these verses, "Chill out. Be at ease. I've got your back. You're in." In the book of Romans, written by the great apostle Paul along with many, many other Pauline letters, Paul explains what the kingdom of God means. Paul sort of keys off of Matthew 6:33 concerning the kingdom of God. Over in Romans 14:17, Paul tells us what the kingdom of God is not. It is not meat and drink but righteousness, peace, and joy in the Holy Ghost. And for he who in these things serves Christ is acceptable to God and approved of men. Hallelujah!

In the body of Christ, there are not many believers who actually know what the kingdom of God literally is. Both Jesus and Paul told us basically the exact same thing, perhaps using different words but essentially the same thing. Jesus was basically saying in Matthew 6:31–34 that the kingdom of God did not consist of what one would eat, drink, or wear as the gentiles or pagans or essentially nonbelievers believe, for your heavenly Father knows already before you ask. Paul was fundamentally saying in Romans 14:17 that the kingdom of God does not pertain to food and drink but righteousness, peace, and joy in the Holy Ghost. What a revelation; what a disclosure. Did I hear both Jesus and Paul declare basically the same thing—that the kingdom of God does not consist of meat, drink, and clothing but of righteousness, peace, and joy in the Holy Ghost? After viewing what both Jesus and Paul had to say about the kingdom of God, I am fundamentally convinced that they are basically right with their observation and assessment. They are right on target. Seek the kingdom of God and his righteousness and all of these things shall be added unto you.

I do not know about you, but as for me and my house, we will serve the Lord (Joshua 24:15). We as believers always must strive to serve God. Since this is the final chapter of my book, let me leave you with a word of exhortation. No matter whatever you do as a saint, believer, follower, disciple, or Christian, never, ever cease from seeking God's kingdom first. Jesus could not emphasize enough the need to seek God's kingdom first; it is very significant that we first seek the kingdom of God with all of our hearts, souls, minds, and strength. How do we seek first God's kingdom? It is by sight, observation, vision, and faith. As the Bible declares in the book of Hebrews 11:6, without faith it is impossible to please God. Therefore, if we are going to seek the kingdom of God first, it must be done according to the measure of faith God has given us.

First and foremost, our faith plays a key or pivotal role in our communication through prayer to our heavenly father on a daily basis. We as believers are the very instrument of both faith and prayer. In all of the Bible, whether Old Testament or New Testament, there is nothing quite like Matthew 6:33, especially when God the Son is doing the communication. Hallelujah! Jesus is communicating to all of his disciples of all generations what their focus or objective should be without a doubt.

The word *but* is a preposition utilized for emphasis or to stress or to underscore a point. First denotes top priority or main focus. As I continue to break down Matthew 6:33 word by word to underscore its importance, seek suggests to look for, to pursue, or to search a continuation. The word *ye* is an old English word for you. Once again, what a revelation, insight, discernment, etc.—a rhema *word*. Psalm 24:1 says the earth is the Lord's and the fullness thereof; it all belongs to God, Jehovah. The kingdom of God denotes or points out that invisible or unseeable person has a kingdom or realm or domain. Matthew 6:33 continues by saying of his very own. And now he is inviting all of us through God the Son to literally seek, search, pursue the kingdom of God, Jehovah. And yet, it is still a simplistic understanding of Matthew 6:33. His righteousness denotes Jehovah's righteousness, not man's righteousness, which is likened to a filthy rag with no real value or worth to God (Isaiah: 64:6). And all of these things shall be added unto you. What is God saying by making such a wonderful, marvelous, and tremendous statement? He's saying, "Whatever you lack, I have, and that's everything."

The question may be asked, "What is the kingdom of God?" The apostle Paul went through the painstaking task of working out a definitive answer for all of us (in the book of Romans). According to scripture, in Romans 14:17 the apostle Paul defined the kingdom of God as righteousness, peace, and joy in the Holy Ghost. The Bible declares in 2 Corinthians 5:21 that we are the righteousness of God predicated on Jesus's death, burial, and resurrection. Hallelujah! The Bible also states that in John 14:27 Jesus, speaking to his disciples, told them this peace (*shalom*) I give and world can't take it. And finally there is joy in the Holy Ghost. The decree is that the joy of the Lord is my strength (Neh. 8:10). Thank you, Jesus! As I have declared in my writings about the kingdom of God and his righteousness, after seeking God's kingdom, everything else falls right into place. The key to perfect balance/harmony as a follower of Jesus Christ is seeking God's kingdom and his righteousness and everything will soon follow.

Printed in the United States
By Bookmasters